125 Brain Games for Babies:

Simple Games to Promote Early Brain Development, Revised

by Jackie Silberg
with contributions from
Keith Pentz
Illustrated by Kathi Dery

Also by Jackie Silberg:

125 Brain Games for Toddlers and Twos: Simple Games to Promote Early Brain Development, Revised

300 Three Minute Games: Quick and Easy Activities for 2–5 Year Olds

500 Five Minute Games: Quick and Easy Activities for 3–6 Year Olds

All About Me

Baby Smarts: Games for Playing and Learning

Brain Games for Babies, Toddlers, and Twos: 140 Fun Ways to Boost Development

The Complete Book of Activities, Games, Stories, Props, Recipes, and Dances for Young Children: Over 600 Selections, with Pam Schiller

The Complete Book of Rhymes, Songs, Poems, Fingerplays, and Chants: Over 700 Selections, with Pam Schiller

Games to Play with Babies, 3rd Edition

Games to Play with Toddlers, Revised

Games to Play with Two-Year-Olds, Revised

Go Anywhere Games for Babies

Hello Rhythm: Rhythm Activities, Songs, and Games to Develop Skills

Hello Sound: Creative Music Activities for Parents and Teachers of Young Children

Higglety, Pigglety, Pop! 233 Playful Rhymes and Chants

The I Can't Sing Book: For Grownups Who Can't Carry a Tune in a Paper Bag… But Want to Do Music with Young Children

I Live in Kansas

I Love Children Songbook

Learning Games: Exploring the Senses Through Play

The Learning Power of Laughter

Let's Be Friends

Lollipops and Spaghetti Activity Book: Developmental Activities

My Toes Are Starting to Wiggle and Other Easy Songs for Circle Time

Peanut Butter, Tarzan, and Roosters Activity Book

Reading Games

Sing Yeladim

Sniggles, Squirrels, and Chickenpox: 40 Original Songs with Activities for Early Childhood

Songs to Sing with Babies

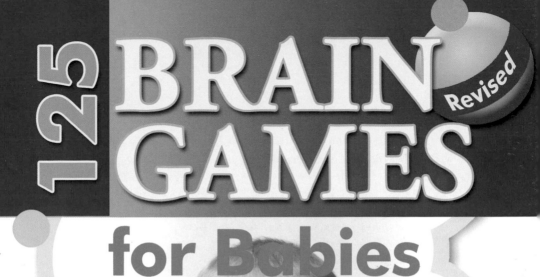

125 BRAIN GAMES

Revised

GAMES

for Babies

Jackie Silberg

with Contributions from **Keith Pentz**

©2012 Jackie Silberg

Published by Gryphon House, Inc.
PO Box 10, Lewisville, NC 27023
800.638.0928; 877.638.7576 (fax)

Visit us on the web at www.gryphonhouse.com.

The author of this book, Jackie Silberg, is an acclaimed speaker, teacher, and trainer on early childhood development and music. You can arrange to have her speak, present, train, or entertain by contacting her through Gryphon House, PO Box 10, Lewisville, NC 27023, 800.638.0928, or at jsilberg@interserv.com.

Cover photograph courtesy of iStockphoto

Illustrations by Kathi Dery

Library of Congress Cataloging-in-Publication Data
Silberg, Jackie, 1934-
125 brain games for babies / Jackie Silberg. -- 2nd ed.
    p.cm.
  ISBN 978-0-87659-391-2 (pbk.)
  1. Ability in infants. 2. Ability in children. 3. Intellect--Problems, exercises, etc. 4. Learning, Psychology of--Problems, exercises, etc. 5. Infant psychology. 6. Child psychology. I. Title.
BF720.A24S57 2012
649'.122--dc23   2011049681

Bulk Purchase
Gryphon House books are available for special premiums and sales promotions as well as for fund-raising use. Special editions or book excerpts also can be created to specifications. For details, contact the Director of Marketing at Gryphon House.

Disclaimer
Gryphon House, Inc. cannot be held responsible for damage, mishap, or injury incurred during the use of or because of activities in this book. Appropriate and reasonable caution and adult supervision of children involved in activities and corresponding to the age and capability of each child involved is recommended at all times. Do not leave children unattended at any time. Observe safety and caution at all times.

Table of Contents

6 to 9 Months

9 to 12 Months

References and
Resources

125 Brain Games for Babies

Introduction

Your beautiful, precious newborn is here! So fragile, so innocent, and so sweet—what can you do to help your baby grow and develop? When do you talk to him, rock him, and sing to him? The answer is **every day**! When will she be able to understand what you are saying? When will she recognize who you are? The answer is **now**!

Every time you talk to, rock, sing to, and touch your baby, you are helping his brain develop. The neurons in your baby's brain are connecting and becoming pathways.

There are many things that a newborn baby can already do:

- Focus on faces that are within eight inches of her face;
- Recognize your voice and turn his head toward the sound of your voice;
- Respond to being touched;
- Suck;
- Yawn, sneeze, and hiccup;
- Grasp things that are placed in her hands; and
- Communicate with crying.

By the time a child is three years old, the brain has formed one thousand trillion connections—about twice as many as adults have. Some brain cells, called neurons, are hardwired to other cells before birth. They control the baby's heartbeat, breathing, and reflexes and regulate other functions essential to survival. The rest of the brain connections are waiting to be "hooked up." The connections that neurons make with other neurons are called synapses. One single brain cell can be connected to more than ten thousand other cells. While parts of the brain develop at different rates, study after study has shown that the peak production period for synapses is from birth to about age 10. During this time, the brain's weight triples to nearly adult size. Scientists believe the stimulation that babies and young children receive determines which connections form in the brain.

How Does the Brain Know Which Connections to Keep?

This is where early experience comes into play. Through repetition, brain connections become permanent. Conversely, a connection that is not used at all, or often enough, is unlikely to survive. For example, a child who is rarely spoken to or read to in the early years may have difficulty mastering language skills later on. Or, a child who is rarely played with may have difficulty with social adjustment as she grows. A child's brain thrives on feedback from his environment. The brain wires itself into a thinking and emotional organ that is formed by what the child experiences. Chances are a child who has a language-rich environment will learn to speak very well. A baby whose coos are met with smiles rather than apathy will likely become emotionally responsive.

The care that an infant receives will have definitive and long-lasting effects on how he will develop and learn, cope with stress, and manage his emotions. Babies thrive when they receive warm, responsive early care.

Scientists continue to learn more each year about how the human brain works! We know that early childhood experiences profoundly shape babies' brains. Research also supports the long-held beliefs that an individual's capacity to learn and thrive in a variety of settings depends on the interplay between nature (her genetic endowment) and nurture (the kind of care, stimulation, and teaching she receives), and that the human brain is uniquely constructed to benefit from experience and from good teaching, particularly during the first years of life.

The very best way to develop babies' brain connections is to give babies what they need, which is an environment that is interesting to explore, that is safe, and that is filled with people who will respond to their emotional and intellectual needs by singing to them, hugging them, talking to them, and reading to them. All these interactions develop the brain's potential for future learning.

All the games in this book develop babies' brain capacity. They are the building blocks of future learning—a good, solid beginning for babies. And they are fun, too!

Revising this book has been an eye-opening experience for me as I learned all the new brain research. There are several new books mentioned in the bibliography that provide the latest information.

I'm forever grateful for the opportunity to learn about our precious little ones and how their brains grow. I've always believed that babies who are 10 days old are just as intelligent as college graduates. They just don't have the ability to express themselves yet and lack experiences to build on. Play the games in this book with your baby, and I bet you will agree with me!

Birth to 3 Months

Newborn Games

- Newborns recognize the voices of their parents. If you patted your tummy and talked to your baby while she was in the womb, she will know the sound of your voice.
- While your infant is on her back, walk to one side and softly call out her name.
- Keep saying her name until she moves her eyes or her head toward the sound of your voice.
- Walk to her other side, and say her name again.
- Gently massage her body as you smile into her eyes and say her name.

What brain research says

The more gentle stimulation you give an infant, the greater the number of brain synapses that are formed.

Heartbeat Sounds!

- Hold your baby against your chest so he can hear and feel your heartbeat.
- Pay attention to your own breathing and the breathing of your baby.
- Let your baby experience the feeling of skin-to-skin contact and the natural rhythms of your body.

What brain research says

While in utero, babies hear and internalize the rhythmic patterns they hear. Your baby will feel comforted and soothed by the natural, rhythmic sounds of your breathing and heartbeat.

Falling in Love

- Make eye contact and body contact with your baby as long as she seems to enjoy and desire it.
- Hold your baby in your arms, and rock her back and forth.
- Say your baby's name and "I love you."
- Make sure your baby experiences many moments of being held, talked to, comforted, and soothed.

What brain research says

Nurturing and loving your baby from the moment of birth helps establish her emotional well-being and her responses to later life experiences.

Baby Talk

- When you speak "parentese" (talking in a high-pitched voice) to infants, you are communicating with them and encouraging their vocal responses. This way of talking to babies develops their language skills.
- Say things such as, "You're such a sweet baby" or "Look at those 10 little toes" in parentese.
- As you speak, hold your baby close to your face, and look directly into his eyes.
- Sing, laugh, and make funny noises, too, to attract your baby's attention.

What brain research says

Babies respond to "parentese"— the high-pitched voice adults use when talking to babies. In addition, infants' brain circuits for hearing benefit when they hear a variety of tones, pitches, and sounds.

The Blowing Game

- This game helps an infant become aware of the different parts of her body.
- Blow gently on your baby's palms. As you blow, say the following words in a singsong chant:

  Here are the baby's palms.

- Kiss your baby's palms.
  - Blow on other parts of her body, and then name those parts of her body in the chant. Most babies like gentle blowing on their elbows, fingers, necks, cheeks, and toes.

What brain research says

Experiences using the five senses help build the connections that guide brain development. Early experiences have a decisive impact on the actual architecture of the brain.

Here's My Finger

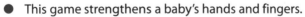

- This game strengthens a baby's hands and fingers.
- Hold your infant in your lap, facing you.
- Hold your index finger in front of your baby's face.
- He probably will grasp your finger, as this is a natural reflex with newborns.
- Each time he grasps your finger, say positive words such as, "That's my wonderful boy!" or "You're so strong!"
- This game also develops tracking skills.

What brain research says

The simple act of reaching for an object helps the brain develop eye-hand coordination.

Hello

- When your baby sees your face, she will be content.
- Say the following poem with your face about eight to twelve inches from your baby's face:

Hello, hello, I love you very much.
Hello, hello, my fingers they can touch.
Hello, hello, I'll touch your little nose. (Touch baby's nose.)
Hello, hello, I'll kiss your little nose. (Kiss baby's nose.)

- Repeat this poem and change the last two lines to different parts of your baby's face—ears, eyes, cheeks, lips.

What brain research says

At birth, babies see best if objects are between eight and twelve inches from their eyes.

Where Did It Go?

- Hold a brightly colored scarf in front of your baby.
- Slowly move the scarf around, and talk about how bright it is.
- When you are sure that your baby is looking at the scarf, slowly move it to one side.
- Keep moving the scarf back and forth to encourage your baby to follow it with his eyes or eventually to try reaching for and grasping the scarf.

  Note: As with any game, watch for signs that your baby may be tired of the game and ready to rest or play something different. Some of the signs are yawning, not being interested in the game, crying, and restlessness.

What brain research says

Neurons for vision begin forming during the first few months of life. Activities that stimulate babies' sight will ensure good visual development.

Follow the Action

- Babies love to look at faces, especially faces of people they love.
- Try different facial expressions and sounds to develop your baby's vision and hearing.
- Here are some ideas:
  - Sing a song, and use big movements with your mouth.
  - Blink your eyes.
  - Stick out your tongue.
  - Make contortions with your mouth.
  - Make sounds with your lips such as smacking your lips.
  - Cough or yawn.

What brain research says

By two months, babies can distinguish features on a face. As your baby's brain grows, this kind of game will help develop her sense of humor.

The Hat Game

- Your face is one of the first things your baby recognizes.
- Try playing this hat game with your infant. When he recognizes your face, you will be stimulating his vision.
- Select different hats to put on your head. As you put on the different hats, say the following:

  Hats, hats, hats, hats; (Slowly shake your head back and forth.)
  (Mommy, Daddy, name of person) has a hat.
  (same person) loves (name of baby) When he wears his hat.

- If you don't have many hats, put a scarf or ribbon on your head.

What brain research says

A one-month-old baby can see as far away as three feet and is very interested in the environment.

Sensory Experiences

- Exposing your baby to many different sensations will broaden her awareness of herself and the world.
- Try gently rubbing your baby's arms with different fabrics. Satin, silk, wool, and terrycloth are good fabrics to start with.
- Give your baby an opportunity to experience different smells. Go outside and smell a flower, or enjoy the smell of a freshly cut orange.
- Talk to your baby about the various sights, sounds, smells, and textures around her.

What brain research says

What babies see and smell create brain connections. The external senses—vision, hearing, smell, and touch—drive emotional responses, which, in turn, eventually will have an impact on learning.

Shadows

- Infants wake up many times during the night.
- Shadows cast on the wall by a nightlight make interesting shapes and forms for your baby to look at.
- If you can arrange a mobile so that it casts shadows, you will be helping your baby's visual development.
- When your child gets a little older, make shadow designs with your hands for your baby to watch.

What brain research says

The neurons for vision begin forming during the first few months of life. Stimulating your baby's vision will help make visual connections in the brain.

Daydream Believer

- Sometimes babies need a little downtime.
- If your baby is awake and alert, sometimes it's good to let your baby just "daydream."
- Give your baby opportunities for quiet personal time to take in and absorb everything that is going on in his environment.
- Times of being entertained and times of stimulating baby's senses need to be alternated with periods of quiet.

What brain research says

Although a baby's brain requires lots of stimulation to create learning and memory pathways and connections, the brain also requires periods of rest in order to consolidate these connections.

Bicycle

- Put your baby on her back, and move the baby's legs like she is riding a bicycle. **Note**: Never force your baby's legs. If your baby resists, try something else.
- Try making up a simple song. Here's an idea that can be sung to the tune of "Row, Row, Row Your Boat":

Ride, ride, ride your bike
Up and down the street.
Happily, happily, happily, happily,
This is such a treat.

- Watch for your baby's reactions, and mimic her coos, gurgles, and smiles.

What brain research says

An infant's brain thrives on feedback from the environment and "wires" itself into a thinking and emotional organ based on her early experiences.

Bend Those Knees

- Place your baby on his back, and carefully pull both legs until they are straight.
- When his legs are straight, tap the bottoms of his feet lightly.
- He will point his toes downward and bend his knees.
- As you do this game, sing the following to the tune of "Ring-around-the-Rosy":

Bending, bending, bending
Little knees are bending
Bending, bending
Hip hooray!

- End the rhyme with some kind of a cheer. Your baby will learn to anticipate it, and it makes the game more exciting.

What brain research says

Physical movement stimulates not only muscle and bone development but also brain growth and development. Research demonstrates that physical activity stimulates the brain to develop connections and pathways between neurons. Active neurological pathways are critical to intellectual and cognitive growth.

Working Out Together

- While your baby is on her back, face your baby and grasp the top corners of the blanket and carefully pull your baby up toward you—and then lower her back down. Make sure you are holding the blanket securely and your baby's head and body are supported.
- Gently move other parts of your baby's body in time to music or a song that you sing.

What brain research says

Physical activity and movement help stimulate brain growth and help neurons make connections for learning. Regular exercise and participation in all forms of physical activity are critical for babies' healthy brain development.

Mouth Sounds

- Hold your baby in your arms.
- Look into his eyes, and stick out your tongue. While it is sticking out, make silly noises.
- Put your tongue back in your mouth.
- Repeat the above, and make a different sound. For example, this time softly smack your lips.
  - Very young babies will often try to stick out their tongues and mimic what they observe and hear.

What brain research says

Talking to your baby starts "wiring" the neurons from his ears to connect with the auditory part of his brain. Babies also identify with facial expressions and mouth sounds. Mimicking or copying your sounds and expressions is the beginning stage of the art of conversation.

Diaper Songs

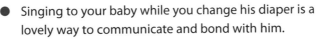

- Singing to your baby while you change his diaper is a lovely way to communicate and bond with him.
- Smile while you are singing.
- Sing any song you know, or sing the following to the tune of "London Bridge Is Falling Down":

Change a diaper, just like this
Just like this,
Just like this.
Change a diaper, just like this.
Clean, clean, baby.

What brain research says

Some of the first circuits that the brain builds are those that govern emotions. Providing loving care will give your baby's brain the right kind of emotional stimulation.

We Are the World

- Talk to your baby about everything. If you know more than one language, speak both languages to your baby.
- If you have relatives or know someone else who speaks another language, encourage those persons to speak to your baby in that second language.
- Speaking to your baby can be done with songs, rhymes, books, or just going over routine tasks.

What brain research says

Infants are born "citizens of the world" with regard to language. Newborns can distinguish sounds from a language, even if they have never heard the language before. By the end of the first year, babies become "language specialists," and the ability to attend to sounds from other languages diminishes greatly. When babies hear more languages, this experience makes a difference in their language development.

A Diaper Game

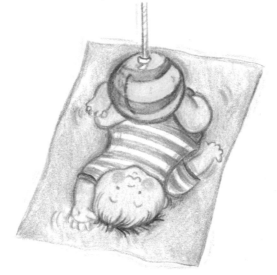

- The changing table is always a good place for developing motor skills.
- Why not give your baby interesting things to look at while he is being changed?
- Try hanging an inflatable ball from the ceiling, close enough for you to reach.
- Make the ball move slowly while you are changing the diaper.
- Your baby will be fascinated by this and, before long, will try to reach out and touch the ball.
- After changing your baby's diaper, hold your baby and let him touch the ball.
- You could also hang a mobile with family pictures from the ceiling.

What brain research says

This game demonstrates the popular viewpoint that babies learn to move their bodies in a sequence that starts from the head and moves down. Researchers have used this progression as a window into early brain development.

Crisscross

- Offer your baby a rattle, toy, or other object for play.
- Watch and encourage your baby to reach and extend when trying to grab and grasp the object. Particularly encourage your baby to cross her midline (any movement of the body or body part that crosses the center or midline of the body that runs from head to toe).

What brain research says

Crossing the midline of the body improves the vestibular sense—the understanding of where the body is and how the body moves through space.

Roll, Roll

- Large inflatable balls are wonderful props to use with infants.
- One way to use this kind of ball is to place your baby on the ball.
- With his tummy on the ball and your hands holding him securely, roll the ball back and forth a little bit.
- While you are rolling, sing a song such as the following, sung to the tune of "Row, Row, Row Your Boat":

Roll, roll, roll the ball
Back and forth we go.
Merrily, merrily, merrily, merrily
Back and forth we go.

- This rocking motion is very relaxing for an infant.

What brain research says

Simple activities such as rocking babies stimulate their brains to grow.

Soothing Smells

- According to Alan Greene, MD, clinical professor of pediatrics at Stanford University School of Medicine, author of a number of books and founder of DrGreene.com, babies develop a sense of smell while still in the womb.
- You can use smells to soothe your baby. Take a nightgown or another piece of your clothing, and secure it close to where she sleeps.
- The smell of "Mom" will comfort her greatly.
  - Pleasant odors such as lavender can also be very soothing.

What brain research says

Newborns orient themselves by smell more than any other sense.

Developing Touch

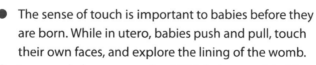

- The sense of touch is important to babies before they are born. While in utero, babies push and pull, touch their own faces, and explore the lining of the womb.
- Lay your baby on your chest. This helps regulate his breathing and body temperature.
- As you hold him close, say loving words and sing songs that you sang when he was in the womb.

What brain research says

Touch is a fundamental and important source of security to an infant. If you deprive an infant of touch, the body and brain stop growing in a healthy manner. Physical stroking helps premature babies to gain weight more quickly and helps healthy babies digest food better. Babies cry less when they are held and carried regularly. Touch is an infant's lifeline to security, attachment, and reassurance.

Up, Down, All Around

- Sit in a chair, and hold your baby in your arms.
- Gently lift one of her arms up and down five times. Count as you lift her arm.
- Now repeat with the other arm.
- Repeat with each of her legs.
- When you are finished, say the following poem:

One, two, three, four, five,
Exercise is fun!
One, two, three, four, five,
You're my honey bun.

What brain research says

Physical activity enhances brain function by providing more oxygen to the brain.

What's Your Name?

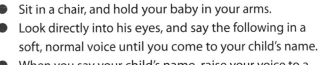

- Sit in a chair, and hold your baby in your arms.
- Look directly into his eyes, and say the following in a soft, normal voice until you come to your child's name.
- When you say your child's name, raise your voice to a higher pitch.

You're so sweet.
You're my baby.
What's your name?
(Say your child's name in a higher voice.)

- Keep repeating this as long as your baby is looking at your face.

What brain research says

When you raise the pitch of your voice, your child's brain receives chemical and electrical impulses.

Connecting Neurons

- Speaking directly to your baby will cause many of her neurons to connect to each other.
- Hold your baby close, and say loving words in a soft and loving voice. A few examples of things to say include the following:

    - You are very special.
    - I love you very much.
        - You are a wonderful baby.

    - Each time you say a loving sentence, give her a gentle squeeze against your body.

What brain research says

The repetition of positive interactions helps the brain reinforce existing connections and makes new connections as well.

Repeating Sounds

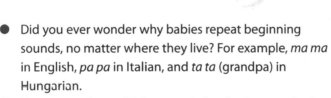

- Did you ever wonder why babies repeat beginning sounds, no matter where they live? For example, *ma ma* in English, *pa pa* in Italian, and *ta ta* (grandpa) in Hungarian.
- New research says it's because infant brains are wired to respond to repetitive patterns.
- Hold your baby in your arms and, as you rock him back and forth, repeat the same syllable over and over. For example, *ma, ma, ma; bo, bo, bo;* or any other initial sound.
- You can also sing or hum the repeating sounds.
- This activity will help develop his language skills.

What brain research says

Newborns' temporal and left frontal areas of the brain are activated whenever they hear repeated sounds.

Tummy Time

- Put your baby on her tummy as often as you can during the day.
- Get down to her level, and talk to her face-to-face.
- Say sweet, loving things, and sing songs.
- Your baby needs to be on her tummy to develop her core muscles.

What brain research says

Research says that it is crucial for infants' core muscles to be allowed to self-activate. Infants develop physically from the neck down, meaning that the upper body, arms, and core muscles get stronger before the legs.

3 to 6 Months

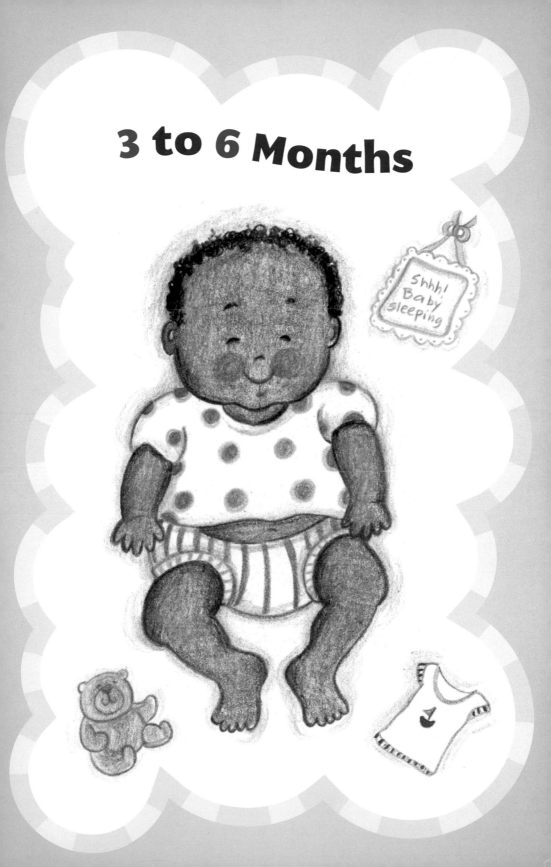

Look What I See

- Babies love to stare at interesting faces and toys.
- Take several colorful toys and, one at a time, slowly move them back and forth in front of your baby to stimulate his vision.
- This is also the time when babies discover their hands. They watch and watch and finally discover that they can make their hands appear in front of their faces and then "disappear."
- Take your baby's hands and gently clap them in front of his face. As you do this, say the following poem:

Clap, clap, clap your hands,
Clap your hands together.
Put your hands on Mommy's face. (Or use the name of the person doing the rhyme.)
Clap your hands together.

What brain research says

Neurons for vision begin forming between the second and fourth months of life. Visually stimulating activities are important at this age.

Who Is That Baby?

- Sit in front of a full-length mirror with your baby in your lap.
- Ask, "Who is that baby?"
- Wave your baby's hand, and say, "Hi, baby."
- Ask, "Where's the baby's foot?"
- Wave your baby's foot, and say, "Hi, foot."
- Continue asking questions and moving different parts of your baby's body.
- Nod heads, wave bye-bye, clap hands, and move other parts of her body, identifying each part of her body as you make the movement.

What brain research says

Linking verbal and visual stimulation strengthens brain connections.

Sock Magic

- Put your hand inside a sock, and use it as a puppet.
- Let your hand move to make the sock "talk."
- As you talk with the sock puppet, use a different voice, and have the puppet touch your baby while naming a part of his body. For example, "I found a toe." "I found an ear." "I found a nose."
- Repeat as long as your baby seems to be engaged.

What brain research says

Multisensory, playful, and interactive experiences linked with language create profound memory connections in the brain.

Let's Watch

- Think of all the different places that are good for observing the environment.
- If babies can watch things move, they are happy.
- A front loading washing machine or dryer is fun for babies to watch.
- Windows that are close to trees are wonderful watching places, or sit outside with your baby for an amazing experience of stimulation.

  - Watch birds fly from one place to another.
  - Watch cars moving down the street.
  - Watch the branches of a tree blow in the wind.

- Take time to sit with your child and watch together. Having you next to her will give her the comfort and security that she needs to enjoy the wonders of the world.

What brain research says

The loving care and support of an adult provides a baby's brain with positive emotional stimulation.

Giggle Box

- Help your baby know how special he is by imitating and mimicking his sounds.
- When your little one begins to giggle, giggle with him.
- Laugh often, and show spontaneous joy at what your baby can do.

What brain research says

Communicating with a young child, even giggling with him, provides patterns for understanding. Laughter, especially, releases feel-good chemicals in the brain that increase the feelings of attachment and of self-worth.

Where's My Baby?

- This is a game that strengthens the back and neck.
- Lie on your back, and put your baby on your tummy.
- With your hands firmly around her chest, raise your baby in the air and up to your face.
- Say the following, and do the actions:

Where's my baby?
There she is. (Lift her up to your face.)
Where's my baby? (Bring her back down to your tummy.)
There she is. (Bring her back up to your face.)
Where's my baby? (Bring her back down to your tummy.)
Up high, high, high. (Bring her up high over your face.)

What brain research says

Developing strength and balance lays the groundwork for crawling and self-confidence. Movement in a variety of directions provides the experience an infant needs to learn how to balance and gain control over her body.

Uppity Uppity Up

- Exercising your baby's arms and legs will help develop his muscles and motor coordination.
- This is a good game to play when your baby is on his back.
- Gently lift up one leg at a time, and say this rhyme:

Uppity up, uppity up
One, two, down. (Put his foot down.)

Note: Never force any movement. If your baby resists, try this another time.

- Repeat with the other foot.
- Repeat with each arm.
- Do both feet at the same time.
- Then do both arms at the same time.

What brain research says

Exercising helps the brain create the circuits for motor skill development. Repetition strengthens these connections in the brain.

I Can Make Music

- Purchase or make socks or ankle bracelets that have bells—make sure the bells are secure and will not come off.
- As your baby begins to move and kick her feet, the sound of the bells will generally be a pleasant and gently stimulating sound.
- Watch as your baby learns the relationship between kicking her feet and the sound of the bells.
- The mesmerizing sound and action will encourage your baby to move and exercise her feet and legs—the combination of the movements, sounds, and visual aspects of this activity support the understanding of cause-and-effect relationships.

What brain research says

Researchers have found that, at around three months, babies are aware that some of their actions bring about predictable responses.

Baby Bounce

- When your baby begins to use your hands for support to pull himself up, he often will also begin to bounce.
- As your baby bounces, encourage him.
- Attempts to stand and bounce increase the use of the leg muscles and encourage muscle development.

What brain research says

Large muscle development is necessary to create the brain connections for coordination, strength, and control.

Going Up the Escalator

- Hold onto baby's fingers, and gently lift her arms as you say the following rhyme:

  Going up the escalator,
  Up, up, up.
  Going down the escalator,
  Down, down, down.

- Lift your baby's legs, and say the rhyme.
- Continue lifting different parts of your baby's body, saying the rhyme each time.
- Try ending with lifting her up in the air and then putting her down.
- Always give her a kiss on the down part.

What brain research says

Children who are touched lovingly, held, and played with regularly develop brains that are larger and have stronger connections between brain cells than children who do not have these experiences.

Talking Together

- At this age babies often make lots of sounds. Mimic the sounds that your baby makes. Those simple sounds will later turn into words.
- Take the words or sounds that your baby makes, such as *ba ba* or *ma ma*, and turn them into sentences. "Ma ma loves you." "'Ba ba,' says the sheep."
- Penelope Leach, a child development expert and the author of *Your Baby and Child*, says, "Your child may say hundreds of different sounds throughout the day, but if you clap and applaud when he or she says, 'ma ma' or 'da da', your baby will keep repeating those sounds because it makes you happy."
- The more you repeat your baby's sounds, the more your baby will be encouraged to make more sounds.
- This is truly the beginning of a conversation.

What brain research says

A baby whose coos and gurgles are met with smiles is developing emotional responsiveness. The more gentle the stimulation you give an infant, the more strides that are made in his brain development.

Connect with Conversation

- Start a conversation with your baby. Say a short sentence such as, "It is a beautiful day today."
- When your baby responds with some babble or a coo, stop talking and look into her eyes.
- As your baby talks, respond with a nod of your head or a smile.
- This indicates to your baby that you are listening to and enjoying her sounds.
- Continue with another sentence. Always stop and listen to your baby's response.
- This game also teaches your child about taking turns.

What brain research says

Language is fundamental to brain development. Having a conversation with your baby is a great stimulant for the brain. Anytime during the day is a good opportunity to talk with your baby and develop her language.

Ba Ba Baby-O

- Sing any song, using one repeated sound instead of words.
- Pick a sound that your baby is making, probably *ma* or *ba*.
- Sing songs using just those sounds with a few words.
- For example, sing the following to the tune of "Old MacDonald Had a Farm":

Ba ba ba ba ba ba baby
Ba ba ba ba O
Ba ba ba ba ba ba baby
Ba ba ba ba O

- Other tunes that you could use are the ones to "Twinkle, Twinkle, Little Star," "The Muffin Man," and "Humpty Dumpty."
- The more that you repeat the sounds your baby is making, the more sounds your baby will make.

What brain research says

The key to language development in the brain is babies hearing language—lots of it. Children need to hear language from birth, long before they can speak. Toddlers whose mothers spoke with them when they were infants have large vocabularies and a solid basis for developing good communication skills.

Roll Olympics

- Helping your baby roll over from tummy to back will develop his chest and arm muscles.
- This is a fun game to play while encouraging your baby to roll over.
- Put your baby on his tummy on a soft and flat surface. Carpeted floors and the middle of the bed are good for this game.
- Hold up a teddy bear in front of your baby's face, and do antics with the bear. You might say the following poem as you make the teddy bear move around:

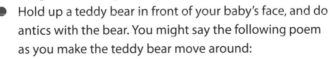

Teddy bear, teddy bear, turn around. (Turn the teddy bear around.)
Teddy bear, teddy bear, touch the ground. (Make the teddy fall down.)

- When you know that your baby is watching the teddy, move it to the side so that your baby's eyes and, hopefully, his body will follow.
- Repeat the poem, moving the teddy bear each time.

What brain research says

Using these muscles repeatedly gives babies' muscles the strength and elasticity for rolling over. Attempts to roll and reach involve cross-lateral movement, which helps develop the vestibular sense.

Pop! Goes the Weasel

- Babies enjoy music and rhythm. When she was in the womb, your baby felt and heard the rhythm of her mother's heart, digestion, breathing, and the sounds of the blood moving in her body.
- Take two rhythm sticks (or two wooden spoons), and tap them together as you sing the song "Pop! Goes the Weasel."
- Tap the sticks softly, and increase the loudness of the sound when you come to the word *pop*.
- Soon your baby will begin to anticipate the louder sound.
- Help your baby hold the sticks. Sing the song while she is holding the sticks:

What brain research says

Exposure to music—listening to, playing, singing—and to rhythm uniquely "wires" neural circuits in the brain.

*All around the cobbler's bench
The monkey chased the weasel.
The monkey laughed to see such fun.
Pop! goes the weasel.*

Let's Bounce

- Bouncing games are such fun for babies, and they play an important role in helping little ones learn balance, a prerequisite for walking.

- You can bounce your baby in many ways—while he is sitting on your lap, lying with his tummy on your knees, or lying on his back on your knees. You can bounce up and down or rock from side to side.
  Note: Always support your baby securely when bouncing him.

- The following are two traditional bouncing rhymes to try:

  To market, to market, to buy a fat pig.
  Home again, home again, jiggity jig.
  To market, to market, to buy a plum bun.
  Home again, home again, market is done.

  I have a little pony, and his name is Dapple Grey.
  He lives down in the stable and not very far away.
  He goes nimble, nimble, nimble.
  He goes trot, trot, trot.
  He goes nimble, nimble, nimble.
  He goes trot, trot, trot.

What brain research says

Bouncing and rocking develop the brain connections needed for crawling and walking.

I Love the Music

- Babies respond in uninhibited ways to sights and sounds.
- If your baby bounces to music or song, help or support her, as needed, and encourage the movement.
- As your baby uses her legs and arms and head movements to respond to stimuli, extend the movements by gently helping to move her arms and legs in even larger motions—including crossing over the body.

What brain research says

Engaging in movement activities in a playful, supportive atmosphere releases neurotransmitters in the brain that activate memory.

Choo-Choo Train

● As you say the following rhyme, move your fingers up your baby's arm and back down again:

Choo-choo train, choo-choo train
Going up the track.
Toot, toot, toot, toot
Now it's coming back.

● Repeat for the other arm.
● Be dramatic with the word *toot*, and soon your baby will be trying to make that sound.

What brain research says

Dramatic speech encourages babies' emotional expression, which activates the brain to release chemicals that help memory.

Swinging

- The action of a swing is very appealing to an infant.
- If you say poems or sing songs as you swing your baby, he will develop a sense of rhythm as well as some very important brain connections.
- Hold your baby in your lap as you swing back and forth.
- Say the following poem as you swing:

Back and forth, back and forth
Swinging, swinging
Back and forth

What brain research says

Infants possess an abundance of genes and brain synapses that are ready to learn or respond to music and poetry.

- Another good poem to say is "The Swing" by Robert Louis Stevenson.

Wiggles and Scoots

- Babies wiggle themselves all over the place. These wiggles and scoots are preparing them to crawl.
- Place your baby on her tummy, and lie on the floor facing her.
- Put an interesting toy in front of her but just out of her reach.
- Move the toy (balls with jingles are good) back and forth.
- As she attempts to get the ball, she will probably scoot forward a little.
- Give her a chance to retrieve the ball, and praise her generously.
- This kind of success develops great self-confidence.

What brain research says

Wiggles and scoots help the formation of the brain synapses that develop future large motor skills.

Push the Baby

- Put your baby down on his stomach.
- Get behind your baby, and place your hands against the soles of his feet.
- When he feels your hands, he will try to bring himself forward by pushing on your hands.
- This is a preparation exercise for crawling.
- Sometimes he will need a gentle push from you.
- While lightly pushing his feet, say the following poem:

Take your little feet and push, push, push. (Gently push your baby's feet.)
Take your little feet and push, push, push. (Gently push your baby's feet.)
Take your little feet and push, push, push. (Gently push your baby's feet.)
Push, push, all day long.

What brain research says

Infants acquire gross motor skills as a result of brain maturation and muscle development. These motor milestones are thought to be hardwired into the brain and develop as long as infants have freedom to practice these skills.

Moving Target

- As your baby lies on her back, show her a soft toy or ball.
- Move the ball near your baby's feet.
- When your baby notices the toy or ball, she will try to kick it.
- Encourage your baby, and talk to her about what she is attempting to do and the name of the object.
- Say, "It's good to kick the ball," or "Can you kick the ball?"
- Let your baby kick the ball. This activity is particularly effective if the object also makes a noise.

What brain research says

Working the leg muscles while observing an object develops eye-foot coordination, a skill that is necessary for certain movements and for spatial awareness.

changing Hands

- When your baby is between three and six months old, he may begin to transfer an object from one hand to the other hand.
- You can help strengthen the neural circuits in his brain by helping your baby practice transferring an object from one hand to the other.
- This game develops small motor skills and eye-hand coordination.
- Put a small rattle into one of your baby's hands.
- Shake the hand with the rattle.
- Show your baby how to transfer the rattle to the other hand. These are the steps:

  - Put your baby's empty hand on the rattle, and he will automatically grab it.
  - Undo your baby's fingers on the first hand from around the rattle, then kiss his fingers.

What brain research says

Learning to transfer objects from one hand to another requires conscious attention. Although hand movements are influenced by touch and sight, these movements must be learned and, therefore, have a strong relationship to cognitive development.

Where's the Toy?

- Hold a favorite toy in front of your baby, and then put it out of sight.
- Encourage her to look for the toy. Ask questions such as, "Is it in the sky?" and then look up to the sky.
- Ask, "Is it on the ground?" and then look down to the ground.
- Ask, "Is it in my hands?" Reply, "Yes, here it is!"
- As your baby learns this game, she will begin to look for the toy when you remove it from her sight.
- Once she has started to pay attention to where the toy goes, she will follow your movements as you put it out of sight.

What brain research says

The experiences that fill a baby's first months of life have a definitive impact on the architecture of the brain and future brain capacity.

Nurturing Curiosity

- Babies are born curious. They are born with an innate drive to understand how the world works.
- When your baby follows a sound by turning his head, it is because he is curious.
- When your baby stares long and hard at a particular object, it is because he is curious.
- Be sure to have colorful pictures on the walls, toys that are safe for your baby to explore, and an interesting environment both indoors and outside.

What brain research says

Nurturing your child's curiosity is one of the most important ways you can help him become a lifelong learner. Neuroscientists have proposed a simple explanation for the pleasure of grasping a new concept: The comprehension triggers a pleasurable response in the brain.

The Scarf Game

- Take a colorful scarf, and swirl it back and forth in front of your baby.
- Throw the scarf up in the air, and watch it float to the ground.
- Try throwing it again and letting it land on your head.
- Throw it in the air, and let it land on a stuffed animal.

What brain research says

Healthy early brain development is more likely to occur in a stress-free, nurturing environment.

Communicating with Your Baby

- How do infants communicate? Through crying, cooing, smiling, and the ways they move their bodies.
- By responding to your baby's expressions, you are telling her that you are paying attention to what she is trying to tell you.
- When you respond, include positive words. Even if she does not understand the words, she will understand the tone of your voice.
  - If your baby is cooing, coo back and say, "I love to hear your voice."
  - If your baby is crying, pick her up and say, "Let's see if we can find out what's the matter."

What brain research says

The human brain is programmed to learn language so we can communicate with one another. Babies have been honing their listening skills since before they were born. After birth, babies begin making sounds that will become words and sentences.

One Thing at a Time

- Maria Montessori believed that young children could not concentrate on more than one thing at a time. If you visit an authentic Montessori classroom, you will see the teacher demonstrating a project without talking. After the teacher finishes demonstrating, then she uses words.
- Overstimulating an infant is very easy to do. Your baby will give you signs that he is being overstimulated.
- Some signs are yawning, closing his eyes, crying, and clasping his hands together.
- If your baby seems to be overstimulated, pick him up, speak softly to him, and hold him close. This will reduce his stress.

What brain research says

The developing brain can only pay attention to one thing at a time.

Learning Words

- Sit at a table with your baby in your lap.
- Put two objects on the table. One could be a baby doll and the other a block.
- As you say the words to your baby, use a high-pitched voice.
- Touch the doll, and say, "baby doll."
- Take your baby's hand, touch the doll, and say, "baby doll."
- Kiss your baby's hand, and say something loving to her.

- Continue with the block.
- Repeat several times.
- Separate the two objects far apart on the table.
- Ask your little one, "Where is the block?" If she doesn't reach for the block or turn her head toward the block, pick up the block or gently turn her head toward the block. Say, "Here's the block!" (if you're holding the block) or "There's the block!" (if you're moving her head).

What brain research says

The way to talk with infants is special. Characteristics of this "parentese" speech include a higher pitch, longer duration, and more exaggerated pitch changes.

Reaching Out

- Sit on the floor with your baby next to you or in your lap.
- Hold an attractive toy in front of him. Hold it just far enough away so that he has to reach out to get the toy.
- As he is reaching, encourage him with a loving and kind voice. When he gets the toy, praise him with your voice and a smile.
- The voice and smile that you use will encourage him to reach out again for other things.
- Play this game many times. Change the toy from time to time to make the game interesting for your baby.

What brain research says

Activity in the brain creates tiny electrical connections called synapses. Repeating the actions that stimulate the brain to make these connections strengthens these connections and makes them permanent.

The Wonders of Music

- Play music for your baby that includes soprano voices.
- Hold her in your arms, and dance around the room.
- Swing, sway, and enjoy the music together.

What brain research says

The womb was your baby's first concert hall. That is where her ears formed within the first 10 weeks of pregnancy. The tones of voice and words that you use help infants feel secure. Talk to your baby in "parentese," with a soft tone of voice, loving words, a higher pitch, and fewer words per phrase. Brain research reveals that "parentese" helps babies focus.

6 to 9 Months

Mirror Games

- It seems that the more a baby sees, the more he wants to see.
- Looking into a mirror is great fun and gives your baby another perspective on who he is.
- Here are some things that you can do with your baby as you look into a full-length mirror:

  - Smile.
  - Shake different parts of the body.
  - Make faces and silly sounds.
  - Make sounds with your lips.
  - Make animal sounds.
  - Rock back and forth.

What brain research says

The neurons for vision begin to connect at birth, so babies need stimulating visual experiences.

Sounds Everywhere

- Expose your baby to a variety of sounds.
- Make sounds with your mouth, and put your baby's fingers on your mouth as you make the sounds.

  - Buzz like a bee.
  - Hum.
  - Pop your cheeks.
  - Make a siren sound.
  - Cough.
  - Pretend to sneeze.

- Crunch different kinds of paper. Cellophane and tissue paper have interesting sounds.

What brain research says

Stimulating babies' auditory development may be the most important sense to develop in the first year. Through hearing, children experience language and music, which stimulate their intellectual and emotional development in ways no other sense can.

Live in Concert

- Babies enjoy sounds and music.
- Show your baby a variety of musical instruments—guitar, bells, triangle, drum, piano, and so on.
- Encourage your baby to touch the instruments.
- If your baby is capable and interested, let her play the instruments to produce sounds, or you can play the instruments for your baby.

What brain research says

The brain likes novelty. By exploring and investigating new things, the brain tries to connect the new experience to an already existing pattern, or the brain creates a new pattern to understand the new experience.

What Did You Say?

- Sing or say a rhyme to your baby that uses a different language than your own.
- If you do not know a song or rhyme in another language, find a relative or friend who does and who would be willing to teach you or come and spend some time singing and talking to your baby.

What brain research says

Hearing the tones and sounds of different languages helps the brain to grow.

Rum Tum Tum

- Babies love to bang with things they hold in their hands. This is excellent for motor coordination and lots of fun, too.
- Sit on the floor with your baby.
- Give your baby a wooden spoon.
- He will need no encouragement to bang the spoon on the floor.
- Sing your favorite songs as you both bang wooden spoons on the floor.
- Try banging spoons to the following poem:

Rum, tum, tum,
Rum, tum, tum,
Bang the drum,
Rum, tum, tum.

What brain research says

The brain refines the circuits needed for reaching and grabbing. Grasping objects helps the brain develop eye-hand coordination and helps muscles learn the patterns of actions. Basic motor skills start developing shortly after birth. Fine motor ability begins developing in the second half of the first year.

Shake It, Baby!

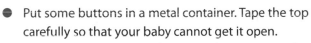

- Put some buttons in a metal container. Tape the top carefully so that your baby cannot get it open.
- Shake the container, and listen to the noise. Watch your baby's eyes grow big with excitement.
- Give the shaker to your baby, and let her shake it as you sing your favorite songs.
- Try singing "Old MacDonald Had a Farm," shaking and making animal sounds together. What could be more fun?
- You can also turn a see-through plastic bottle into a shaker. Your little one will enjoy watching the rocks or buttons move when they are being shaken.

What brain research says

Eric Jensen, author of Music with the Brain in Mind, says that infants possess an abundance of genes and synapses that make them ready to appreciate and learn about music.

One, Two

- Sit with your baby on the floor.
- Make up rhymes as you hold your baby's hand and let him touch different parts of your body.
- Here are some ideas:

  One, two, three, touch my knee.
  Yellow, red, touch my head.
  Dippity dips, touch my lips.
  Apples, pear, touch my hair.

What brain research says

Babies need touching experiences to grow the brain and grow the body; these experiences are just as critical as nutrients and vitamins.

- Each time you say the part of the body, put your child's hand on that part. When you say, "One, two, three, touch my knee," put your baby's hand on your knee.
- Reverse the game, and touch your baby as you say the rhyme.

Tommy Thumb

- Say the rhyme as you touch your baby's fingers one by one:

  Tommy Thumb, Tommy Thumb,
  Where are you?
  Here I am, here I am.
  How do you do?

- Repeat with "Peter Pointer," "Toby Tall," "Ruby Ring," "Sally Small," and "fingers all."
- On the final verse, wave your baby's hand.
- Your baby will respond to your touch and your voice.

What brain research says

Songs and fingerplays provide rich language opportunities that are vital to the development of the brain.

I've Got Power

- Babies enjoy interactive experiences.
- Your baby will eventually initiate a game related to dropping and retrieving.
- When your baby drops an object, retrieve it and give it back to your baby.
- Your baby will soon learn that if she drops something, someone will pick it up.

What brain research says

Dropping objects from a high chair to the floor is practice for the grasp-release skills. Embrace this game! It also helps develop depth perception and sound-distance awareness.

Rolling Along

- Your baby will enjoy playing with a variety of balls.
- Find several small balls that attract the interest of your baby.
- Locate a tube that will allow the balls to pass through readily.
- Roll the balls through the tube. Watch for your baby's surprise and anticipation when he notices the ball coming out of the other end of the tube.
- Describe the action and your baby's response as the balls "disappear" and then "reappear."

What brain research says

Play and playful interactions are critical for the developing brain. Adding an element of surprise and challenge enhances the learning experience.

Puppet Peekaboo

- Children love watching and playing with puppets.
- Put a puppet on your hand, and hold it behind your back.
- Bring out the puppet, and say, "Peekaboo, (child's name)."
- Now put it behind your back again.
- Continue doing this until your baby begins to anticipate the puppet coming out at a certain place.
- Then bring the puppet out at a different place—over your head, over the baby's head. Always bring it down in front of your baby's face (not too close) when you say the peekaboo words.
- Give the puppet to your baby, and see if she will imitate you.

What brain research says

With every game of peekaboo, thousands of connections among brain cells are formed or strengthened, adding a bit more development to the complex "wiring" that will remain largely in place for the rest of the child's life.

I Know You're There—Somewhere

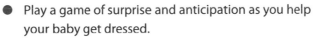

- Play a game of surprise and anticipation as you help your baby get dressed.
- As you put on your baby's shirt, ask a question such as, "Where is my baby?" when your little one's head is covered.
- Quickly say something such as, "There you are," just as soon as you can see your baby's face.
- Modify the questions to include body parts such as feet, toes, legs, fingers, arms, and so on.
- Always act surprised and pleased when you provide a response.

What brain research says

Loving interactions with people and exploring objects are as necessary to a child's brain development as food is.

Ahh-Boom!

- Prop your baby on your lap in a sitting position facing you.
- Lower your head, and gently touch foreheads with your baby while slowly saying, "Ahh-boom!" at each touch.
- In time, your baby will anticipate the game by leaning forward before your foreheads meet.
- Another way to play this game is to stretch out the word *ahhh* and only say the word *boom* when foreheads meet. Babies love this game.

What brain research says

The quality of the relationship an infant has with his parents has a direct impact on the physical development of the brain. Every child deserves a brain boost in his first years!

Surprise! Surprise!

- Your baby enjoys fun and unique experiences.
- Find an object such as a toy that squeaks, a Slinky toy, or another expandable and changeable item.
- Squeeze the toy to make it squeak, expand the Slinky, or demonstrate the changeable characteristics of another item.
- Watch for the surprise and excitement the object provides for your little one.
- Use words, sounds, exclamations, or other means to add to the drama of the moment.

What brain research says

Positive experiences enhance brain connections. Genes provide the brain's "building materials"; the environment builds the brain through trillions of brain cell connections that result from experiencing the world through movement and the senses of sight, sound, smell, and touch.

Peekaboo Fun

- There are so many different kinds of peekaboo games, and babies love them all.
- The favorite is covering your face with your hands and then taking them away.
- This shows your baby that even though she can't see your face, you are still there.
- This game is very important in "wiring" the brain.
- Other ways to play peekaboo:

  - Put your baby's hands over her eyes, and then take them away.
  - Hold a towel or cloth diaper between you and your child. Peek out of the side and the top of the towel or cloth diaper.
  - Toss a towel or cloth diaper over your head, and then take it away.

What brain research says

Although pat-a-cake and peekaboo look like innocent play, these games communicate complex sets of rules about turn-taking and expectations. A developing brain will adapt to whatever happens repeatedly in the environment. For their brains to develop optimally, children need to have fun, interesting, and loving experiences each day.

Peekaboo Music

- Sing this song to the tune of "Frère Jacques":

  Are you sleeping, are you sleeping,
  Little (child's name), *little* (child's name)?
  Now it's time to wake up,
  Now it's time to wake up,
  Ding, ding, dong
  Ding, ding, dong.

- Use this as a peekaboo song.
- Cover your eyes as you sing, "Are you sleeping?"
- When you sing, "Now it's time to wake up," take your hands away from your eyes.
- When you sing, "ding, ding, dong," move your baby's hands up and down as if he is ringing a bell.

What brain research says

Peekaboo games create new brain connections and strengthen existing ones.

The Big Squeeze

- Playing with squeeze toys is great fun. The rubbery kind seem to be the easiest to squeeze.
- Your baby is developing small motor skills when she squeezes things.
- If your baby is having trouble squeezing the toy, put your hands over your baby's hands, and squeeze the toy. Once she gets the feeling of how to squeeze the toy to make the noise, your baby will be able to do it by herself.
- Here is a fun little poem to say as you squeeze the toy:

What brain research says

Exercising small muscles has a positive effect on the motor areas of the brain and prepares the body for future learning.

Squeeze the cheese, Louise, please!
Squeeze the cheese, Louise, please!
Not the bees and not the trees!
Squeeze the cheese, Louise, please!

- Squeeze on the word *please*.

Touching Textures

- Gather together strips of different kinds of materials—wool, cotton, velvet, satin, and any others that you might have.
- Sit on the floor with your baby, and hold out one of the material pieces close enough for him to reach. When he grabs at it, praise his effort.
- Once he has touched the strip of material, tell him the name of it, and place it on his palm. Describe the feel of the material: "This is velvet, and it feels smooth."
- He will not understand all of your words, but he will associate the sound of your voice with the feel of the material.

What brain research says

Games that challenge your baby to reach for an object develop your baby's eye-hand coordination, which impacts the "wiring" in his brain.

Another Pop Game

- Movement and music together stimulate both sides of the brain.
- Hold your baby in your arms as you move around the room and sing to the tune of "Pop! Goes the Weasel."
- When you come to the word *pop*, hold your baby high in the air, and then bring her down for a kiss.

All around the cobbler's bench
The monkey chased the weasel.
The monkey laughed to see such sport.
            Pop! goes the baby (Or say your child's name).

What brain research says

Cross-cultural studies show that infants who receive a generous amount of loving touch throughout the day develop intellectually, emotionally, socially, and physically better than babies who receive less loving touch. Touch is a basic, essential need.

Sing and Say

- Music and rhythm have a powerful effect on brain development.
- Think about the songs you like to sing, and then sing them to your baby.
- Whatever songs you sing, your baby is going to enjoy hearing the words. It doesn't matter that he doesn't understand them.
- If your song has a familiar word that you know your child understands, sing that word louder than the others.
- Instead of singing a song, try saying the words to the song in different ways—whispering them or saying the words in a soft, loud, or high-pitched voice.
- Whether you sing or speak the words, the rhythm will open windows of opportunity in your child's brain.

What brain research says

Understanding music, especially rhythm, involves the interplay of both sides of the brain. Playing many types of music for your baby develops his brain and a sense of pitch, which is critical to his language development.

Abracadabra

- Put a brightly colored scarf inside a paper tube.
- Pull out the scarf, and show delight and surprise.
- Put the scarf back into the tube.
- Invite your baby to pull out the scarf.
  - Observe the surprise and amusement on your baby's face.
  - Your baby will want to play this game again and again!

What brain research says

Novelty and surprise, when they happen in a safe, supportive environment, create learning and memory connections in the brain.

A Goodnight Rhyme

- Rock your baby as you say the following rhyme:

Goodnight, sweet baby. Goodnight, sweet one.
The clock is ticking and says, "We're done."
Goodnight, sweet baby. Goodnight, my dear.
The stars are twinkling, and sleep is near.

- Gently put your baby in her bed, and say, "Goodnight, goodnight."
- Rub your baby's tummy, and give her a kiss.

What brain research says

Holding and cuddling comforts your baby and helps her brain develop and grow.

Love Those Keys!

- Keys are a favorite toy for babies. They make noise and are easy to hold, and babies like to drop them.
- Hold the keys in your hand, and say, "One, two, three, let's drop the keys."
- Drop the keys on the floor, and be sure your little one watches them drop.
- Put the keys in your baby's hand and repeat.
- Open your baby's fingers, and let the keys drop.
- After a few times, your baby will know what to do and will delight in this game.
- This is an excellent game for developing small motor skills.

What brain research says

When your baby exercises the muscles in his hands, the activity stimulates his brain development.

Waving

- Wave your baby's feet and hands to people or pets your baby knows.
- Sing this song to the tune of "Frère Jacques":

Wave to Daddy, wave to Daddy,
Wave, wave, wave,
Wave, wave, wave.

Say hello to Daddy, say hello to Daddy,
Wave, wave, wave,
Wave, wave, wave.

- You can wave with either hands or feet to Mommy, Grandma, Grandpa, friends, and pets.

What brain research says

Brain research scientists have learned that the parent-child attachment is the most critical factor in your baby's development.

Listening Fun

- The more experience that your little one has listening, the better language skills she will have.
- Include your baby as much as you can in family conversations. At the dinner table, listening to others talk will teach her numerous words.
- Remember that even though your baby cannot say the words, she still understands a great deal.
- Play different programs on the radio so your baby hears different voices and sounds.
- Often your baby will respond to what she is hearing. Encourage her responses by interacting with her.

What brain research says

The most intensive period of speech and language development is during the first three years of life. Speech and language skills develop best in an environment that is rich with sounds, sights, and the speech and language of other people.

Reading Tips

- Set aside a special time each day for books. Bedtime is often a good choice.
- Select books with short sentences and simple illustrations.
- Let your baby hold a book and turn the pages.
- Begin by naming the pictures. The story will come later.
- Stop and talk about anything in the book that your baby seems interested in. A picture may remind him of something else. Keep the conversation going, and use lots of descriptive words.
- Most important: repeat, repeat, repeat. Your baby will want to read the same book over and over. The more you repeat, the more you are establishing brain connections.

What brain research says

An infant's brain is "wired" by the repetition of sound, developing strong neural pathways in the brain that become the "highways" of learning.

Let's Climb

- There is no avoiding it! Your baby will begin to climb everything in sight. Why not help her along and develop her large muscles?
- Pile cushions and pillows on the floor.
- Put your baby in front of the pillows, and she will have a wonderful time.
- Put a favorite toy on top of one of the pillows. This will entice her even more.

    Note: Stay close by as your baby explores the environment.

What brain research says

Each young brain forms, at its own pace, the neural and muscular connections required for crawling and climbing.

The Signing Game

- Much research has been done about teaching sign language to babies. Infants who recognize simple signs seem to like books earlier because they have more ways to identify with what they see in a book.
- For example, if you are reading a book to your baby and there is a picture of a cat, you can say the word *cat* and make the sign for *cat*. This additional cue helps your baby make the connection between the word and the picture.
- Here are three simple signs to teach your baby:

  - Cat—take the palm of your hand, and stroke the back of your other hand.
  - Fish—open and close your mouth like a fish.
  - Bird—flap your arms up and down in the air.

- Singing songs that include these words is an excellent way to reinforce the signs. A song such as "Old MacDonald Had a Farm" is a good one to sing.

What brain research says

The brain is capable of learning throughout life, but no other time will ever equal this most productive time of learning.

Upsidoodle

- This fun game is great exercise that also helps babies learn to anticipate when something is going to happen.
- Have your baby lie down on a soft, flat surface.
- Hold his hands and wrists, and count, "One, two, three, upsidoodle."
- Gently pull him up to a sitting position.
- Shout, "Hooray!" when he is sitting.
- Gently lower him back to the lying-down position and repeat.
- After several repetitions, your baby will anticipate the ride up. Again, be sure your baby can support his head and neck before doing this activity.

What brain research says

Healthy early brain development is more likely to occur in a stress-free, nurturing environment.

Rock and Sing

- Put your baby on her tummy, and encourage her to hold her head up high.
- Lie down facing her so you are doing the same thing.
- Get up on all fours, and rock back and forth.
- Encourage your baby to copy you.
- While you are on all fours, rock back and forth and sing or hum a song. It doesn't have to have words; just syllables with a happy tune is fine. This will encourage your baby to hum and rock back and forth on all fours.

What brain research says

Tummy-time activities for babies allow them to develop the head control and upper-body strength they need to crawl. Tummy playtime improves your baby's coordination skills in addition to enhancing her brain development.

Read It Again!

- Nothing is more delicious than snuggling up with your little one to share a book.
- Babies have books that they love. These are the books that they want you to read over and over again. The reasons could be many—the colors, the pictures, the feel of the material (sturdy or soft), the story.
- At this age, your baby will be very interested in looking at the pictures and turning the pages.
  - Use your baby's name in the story wherever possible.
    - Choose books that are highly tactile or textured. Babies this age also respond strongly to sound, so look for books that incorporate elements that crinkle, crunch, jangle, swish, beep, or make music.

What brain research says

Repetition organizes language patterns for babies and helps them understand new words and new meanings of words. Babies begin exploring the world through touch, which may be why touch-related books for babies are so plentiful.

Nose to Nose

- Love and affection are very real needs. Your baby is never trying to manipulate or control you; he simply has a biological need for your love and affection.
- Hold your little one in your arms, and say the following:

  Nose to nose, (Touch noses.)
  Cheek to cheek, (Touch cheeks.)
  Ear to ear, (Touch ears.)
  I love you. (Give your baby a loving hug.)

What brain research says

Unconditional love supports your baby's self-esteem and an increased development of brain circuitry.

Conversational Signing

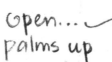

open... → palms up

palms down

- The age of six months is a good time to start doing baby signs with your baby.
- Some of the most important signs you can introduce are *more* (while feeding), *eat, bottle time,* and *all done.*
- You can use American Sign Language (ASL) signs or make up your own signs for each action you are introducing. There are many books about using sign language with babies, or you can use a search engine to find a website that shows signs that can be used with babies.
- The important part is to use the signs consistently.
- Your baby will soon be signing to you.

What brain research says

Conversation exercises the brain. The plasticity of the brain makes it possible for infants to learn another language, such as signing. The more words an infant learns, the more brain connections she will make. Signing gives her a chance to communicate and be part of a conversation.

9 to 12 Months

Outside Exploring

- Playing outside on a lovely day is a wonderful way for your baby to experience with his senses.
- Let your baby crawl in the grass while you crawl along with him.
- Name each thing that your baby seems interested in.
- Smell flowers, tickle with grass, look for bugs, and let your baby explore the environment with his senses. There are so many things to do.
- Rolling over in the grass is fun. Your baby may enjoy the light, prickly feel of the grass.

What brain research says

Early childhood experiences have a dramatic and precise impact, physically determining how the intricate neural circuits of the brain are wired.

Seek and Ye Shall Find

- Listening for the source of a sound is a very good game to develop auditory awareness.
- You will need a wind-up clock that makes a nice ticking sound.
- Hold the clock, and say a little tick-tock rhyme to your baby.

Tick, tock, tick, tock,
Goes the clock,
Tick, tock.

- Now put the clock under a scarf, blanket, or towel.
- Ask your child, "Where is the tick-tock?"
- Help guide her to the clock, using the sound to locate it. Once she understands how to play this game, she will want to do it again and again.

What brain research says

An infant's brain can discern every possible sound in every language. By 10 months, babies have filtered the sounds they hear and have learned to focus on the sounds of their native language.

Where Is _____?

- Sit down with your baby, and look at pictures together.
- Find a picture of someone in your family.
- Talk about the picture by naming the person in it. Say the name again, and ask your baby to point to the person in the picture.
- Now, cover up the picture with your hand, and ask your baby to find the person.
- Continue playing this game with another picture.
- Your baby might surprise you by how much he understands!

What brain research says

A warm, loving relationship with a baby strengthens the brain connections that help him handle emotions.

I Touch

- This rhyme helps your baby identify different parts of her body.
- Have your baby stand and hold on to a chair or another piece of furniture.
- First say the rhyme and point to each part of your body.
- Next, take your baby's hand and point to each part of her body as you say the rhyme again.

I'll touch my chin, my cheek, my chair.
I'll touch my head, my heels, my hair.
I'll touch my knees, my neck, my nose.
Then I'll bend and touch my toes.

- You are also saying words that begin with the same sound.

What brain research says

Touch is critical to development! Of all the sensory experiences, touch is how babies first know that they are loved.

Quite Puzzling

- This is a good time to introduce simple, basic, and easy-to-do puzzles.
- Provide your baby with one-piece or two-piece wooden puzzles with knobs. Make sure the puzzles are easy to put together.
- Talk to your baby as he tries to put the puzzle pieces in the puzzle. If necessary, help him put the puzzle together.
- Celebrate together when your baby accomplishes the task.

What brain research says

Experiences that begin with simple concepts and lead to more complex ideas and solutions are the foundation for neural wiring.

This Is Bill

- Sit on the floor with your baby in your lap.
- Hold one of her ankles in each hand as you say the following rhyme:

This is Bill, and this is Jill.
They went out to play.
Over and over, (Gently move your baby's legs over each other.)
Over and over, (Gently move your baby's legs over in the other direction.)
"This is fun," said Bill and Jill.
And then they said, "Hooray!"
(Give your baby a big hug.)

What brain research says

Positive touch releases hormones and stimulates neurotransmitters that are important for creating memories and fostering learning.

Wash the Toy

- Wet washcloths are wonderful fun for babies. The texture feels good all over his body and especially on his face.
- Play peekaboo with a washcloth when giving him a bath.
- Tuck a small toy in a washcloth, and let your little one put his fingers in the folds of the washcloth to find the toy.
- Give your baby the washcloth, and let him wash your face.
- Show your baby how to wash one of his bath toys with a washcloth.
- Sing the following song to the tune of "Row, Row, Row Your Boat":

What brain research says

Sensory experiences and social interactions with infants build brain connections for future learning.

Wash, wash, wash the ball.
Get it nice and clean.
Scrubby, scrubby, scrubby, scrubby
(Help your child wipe the toy with the washcloth.)
Now it's nice and clean.

All Things New Again

- Wrap a few of your baby's favorite toys in colorful leftover pieces of wrapping paper.
- Present the presents to your baby.
- Watch and observe how your little one uses her hands, eyes, and focus to find out what is hidden under the wrapping paper.
- Describe the toy and act surprised when it is finally revealed: "There's your favorite ball," or "You opened up the present and found your bear."

What brain research says

Through touching, grasping, and manual manipulations, infants learn about the features of people, objects, and their environment. Fine motor development is necessary to be able to feed and dress oneself. Playing with stacking rings, large stringing beads, and puzzles offers opportunities for infants to practice their fine motor skills.

One, Two, Three, Kick

- Show your little one how you can hold on to the side of a chair and kick your leg in the air.
- Encourage him to copy you.
- Say, "One, two, three, kick," and kick your leg in the air on the word *kick*.
- Listening for the word *kick* is a lot of fun for babies, and kicking a leg into the air develops their muscle strength.
- Kick in front, kick to the side, and kick in back.
- Try counting in a soft voice and saying the word *kick* in a big voice.

What brain research says

Physical movement stimulates not only muscle and bone development, but also brain growth and development. Research shows that physical activity stimulates the brain to develop connections and pathways between neurons. Active neurological pathways are critical to intellectual and cognitive growth.

Rolling

- Show your baby how to make a fist.
- Gently roll her fists over each other as if you were doing pat-a-cake.
- As you roll her fists, say the following rhyme:

    Rolling, rolling, little hands,
    Rolling down the street.
    Rolling slowly, (Roll her hands slowly.)
    Getting faster, (Pick up the speed.)
    Roll, roll, roll, roll, roll. (Roll faster and faster.)

- End with a big hug and kiss.

What brain research says

Brain research shows that babies need nurturing and secure relationships. They also need a stimulating environment with opportunities for exploring and for problem solving.

Silly Antics

- Developing an awareness of his capabilities is something that you can encourage in your baby.
- Sit on the floor with your baby facing you.
- Do a variety of silly things, and encourage him to imitate you. Here are some ideas:

  - Make a funny face.
  - Stick out your tongue, and make silly sounds.
  - Move your head in different directions, up and down and side to side.
  - Pound your fists on your chest and yell.
  - Make different animal sounds.
  - Lie on your back, and kick your legs in the air.
  - Get on your hands and knees, and bark like a dog.

- After you have done several things that your baby has imitated, repeat them in front of a mirror. When your baby sees himself doing the antics, he will have even more fun.

What brain research says

Expressing emotions activates chemicals in the brain that heighten memory.

Fun with Stacking Toys

- Stacking-ring toys have lots of possibilities for developmental play.
- Depending on your baby's developmental needs and skills, encourage her to try any of the following:

  - Stacking the rings large to small, small to large, and any old way
  - Throwing the rings
  - Putting the rings on her fingers
  - Putting the rings in her mouth
  - Spinning the rings

- All toys have great creative possibilities. Help your baby see different ways to play with toys.

What brain research says

Helping a baby's brain grow means immersing her in environments that are emotionally and intellectually rich and stimulating.

Humpty Dumpty

● Say this popular nursery rhyme as you bounce your baby on your knees.

Humpty Dumpty sat on a wall. (Bounce baby.)
Humpty Dumpty had a great fall. (Open your knees and, while holding your baby securely, let him slide down to the ground.)
All the kings horses and all the kings men
Couldn't put Humpty together again. (Bring baby back up to your knees.)

What brain research says

Songs, movement, and musical games of childhood have been called brilliant neurological exercises that introduce children to speech patterns, sensory motor skills, and essential movement skills.

● Give your baby a favorite stuffed animal to hold as you play this game.
● This may give him the idea to play the game with his stuffed animal.
● When you see him playing the game, you know there has been a connection in the brain.

'Round and 'Round

- Your baby enjoys much interaction.
- Whether your baby is crawling or beginning to walk, a simple game of going after her in a type of chase will keep your little one excited.
- Move in a manner similar to how your baby moves.
- Add vocal calls, sounds, encouraging words, or other noises to keep the connection.
- If your little one chooses to, let her crawl or walk to chase you, too.

What brain research says

Infants learn about themselves and their world during interactions with others. Brain connections that lead to later success grow out of nurturing and supportive care. This type of care fosters children's curiosity, creativity, and self-confidence. Young children need safety, love, conversation, and a stimulating environment to develop and keep important synapses in the brain.

Copy Me

- Developing large motor skills will help babies make brain connections.
- Do an action, and ask your child to copy you. If he doesn't understand what "copy me" means, move his body to copy what you do.
- Try looking in a full-length mirror as you play this game.
- Here are some actions that you can do:

  - Take giant steps—if your child isn't walking, do it crawling.
  - Take little steps—if your child isn't walking, do it crawling.
  - Hold one arm out to the side, and make big circles.
  - Make circles with the other arm.
  - Hold a large beach ball, then drop it and pick it up.

What brain research says

Most scientists now agree that motor skills develop when the brain has been "wired" for the task by learning and practicing new movements.

Let's Pull

- This game develops upper-arm strength, and your baby will absolutely adore it.
- Sit on the floor facing your baby.
- Take one end of a long scarf, and give the other end to your baby.
- Start gently pulling the scarf, and show your baby how to pull back.
- When she begins to pull hard, fall over. This is often hilarious to babies.
- This game is excellent for muscle development and lots of fun to play.

What brain research says

The critical period for muscle control begins shortly after birth. This period lays the foundation of brain circuits dedicated to motor control. Physical activity is a strong determinant in the early development of the brain.

Fast and Slow Rhythms

- Give your baby some wooden spoons or rhythm sticks.
- Put your little one in a high chair, or have him sit on the floor.
- You should have some wooden spoons or rhythm sticks, too.
- Sing a song such as "The Wheels on the Bus," and tap the sticks to the beat of the song.
- Encourage your baby to tap his sticks, too.
- Sing the same song faster, and tap your sticks faster.
- Sing the song slowly, and tap your sticks slowly.
- Your baby will enjoy watching you tap the sticks faster and slower and will begin to understand the concepts of *fast* and *slow*.

What brain research says

Early music experiences increase and enhance spatial-temporal reasoning and the learning of mathematical concepts.

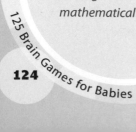

Mouth Songs

- As your baby is developing language skills, she will enjoy discovering all the many sounds that she can make with her mouth.
- Pick a song that your little one enjoys hearing. Some popular ones are "The Itsy, Bitsy Spider," "This Old Man," and "Twinkle, Twinkle, Little Star."
- Sing the song in different ways. Hum it, sing it in a high voice, a whispering voice, and any other voice that you think your child will enjoy hearing.
- The more ways your baby hears this song, the more she will try to copy you and develop her language skills.

What brain research says

Songs, movement, and musical games of childhood are neurological exercises that help children learn speech patterns and motor skills.

New Zoo Revue

- Take your baby to a zoo, and, if possible, to an area where he can pet or touch the animals.
- Talk to your child about the animals you see.
- Mimic the sounds that you and your baby hear.
- Describe the colors, smells, sights, and sounds of the zoo.
- As much as possible, allow your baby to interact with the animals by petting or touching them.

What brain research says

What the five senses experience help the connections that guide brain development. Early experiences have a decisive impact on the actual architecture of the brain.

I'm a Big Kid Now

- At some point your child will offer to care and do for you what you have been doing for her.
- As opportunities present themselves, let your baby offer you food, attempt to wash your face with a washcloth, brush or comb your hair, or do other engaging tasks.
- Talk to your child about what she is doing, and be sure to offer her your thanks.

What brain research says

The circuits that form in the brain fundamentally decide who we are. A baby whose coos are met with smiles and hugs rather than impassivity will likely become emotionally responsive.

Changes

- Play a simple game with your child. It involves a response or reaction to a simple action.
- Puff out your cheeks or one cheek with air and, as your little one pushes on your puffed-out cheek, puff out the other side.
- If your little one touches your nose, open your mouth.
- If your baby pats your head, hum some notes.
- Provide simple responses to interactions initiated by your little one.

What brain research says

The concept of cause and effect is key to brain development in many areas, including your baby's intellectual and social development.

The Teeth Rhyme

- This is one of those games that babies love. It is a lot of fun!
- Teach your baby to open his mouth and show his teeth.
- Stick out your tongue, and see if your little one will copy you.
- Now, rub your tongue against your upper teeth.
- Say the following rhyme, and do the actions:

Four and twenty white horses, (Point to your teeth.)
Standing in a stall.
Out came a red bull, (Stick out your tongue.)
And licked them all. (Lick your upper teeth with your tongue.)

- Say it again, and point to your baby's teeth and tongue.
- Encourage your baby to stick out his tongue and try to lick his upper teeth.
- This can be very funny.

What brain research says

A growing body of scientific evidence shows that the way babies are cared for will determine not only their emotional development, but also the development of their brains and their central nervous systems. Humor is an important part of that development.

Jack in the Box

- This popular game reinforces the idea that surprises can be fun.
- Make fists with both hands, and tuck your thumbs under the fingers.
- Say the rhyme, and on the words "Yes, I will!" pop up your thumbs.

Jack in the box sits so still.
Won't you come out?
Yes, I will!

What brain research says

Rhymes and poems are neurological exercises that introduce children to speech patterns, sensory motor skills, and vital movement strategies.

- Help your child make a fist, and show her how to pop up her thumb.
- You can also play this game by crouching down and jumping up at "Yes, I will!"

Bursting Bubbles

- Blow bubbles for your child.
- Encourage your baby to reach for, touch, poke, smash, or otherwise burst the bubbles.
- Describe the sizes and colors of the bubbles.
- Count the bubbles as they float around the room.

What brain research says

At this age, babies can judge distances well. Their eye-hand and eye-body coordination allows them to grasp and throw objects fairly accurately. Perception skills, such as visual memory and visual discrimination, help babies make sense of their exciting new world.

A Stroller Game

- Take your baby outside, and help him sort out the environment. Even though there is much to see, help him focus on one thing at a time.
- Push the stroller along, and stop at interesting things to talk about.
- Stop at a tree, and talk about the leaves. Let your little one touch the leaves.
- Look for birds or squirrels in the trees.
- Talk about just three or four things on your walk.
- Repeat this experience many times, pointing out the same three or four things before you add new ones.

What brain research says

Through the wonder of positron emission tomography (PET) scans, scientists have learned that the part of the brain that stores memories becomes fully functional at 9 to 10 months.

Discovering Books

- Reading aloud is a wonderful gift that you can give your child.
- Infants are interested in pictures, the shape of the book, turning the pages, and holding and touching the book.
- Point to a picture, and tell what it is. When you point to the same picture several times, your child will learn the name of the object or person.
- Ask your child, "Where is the _____?" See if she will point to the picture.
- Let your baby hold, drop, and turn the pages of a book. This kind of experimentation sets the path for good speech and reading, and offers special times between you and your child.
- Read the same book over and over many times.

What brain research says

The more you talk to and read to your child, the stronger the brain connections related to language will be. Language is key to future academic success.

Grocery Shopping

- Taking your baby to the supermarket can be a pleasant experience.
- Here are some things to do with your baby while at the supermarket:

  - Point out pictures on the cans and boxes.
  - Show your baby the foods that he eats and drinks at home.
  - Give him the opportunity to choose familiar foods.
  - Let him put some of the foods in the grocery cart.
    - Describe foods as you put them in the cart as *hot, cold, soft, chewy, crunchy*, and so on.

What brain research says

The size of a baby's vocabulary is largely determined by what he hears in the first three years of his life. If you talk, sing, and read to your baby, he has a greater chance of having a larger vocabulary when he learns to speak. The brain tunes in to the sounds that make up words and then builds connections that allow it to retrieve the sounds as vocabulary grows.

- The world of language awaits you at your local supermarket.

Mary Mack

- The jump-rope chant "Miss Mary Mack" is fun to say, in part, because the ending word repeats three times.
- Say the rhyme, and on the word that repeats, hold your baby and jump. If your baby can stand, hold her around the waist and help her jump.

Miss Mary Mack, Mack, Mack
All dressed in black, black, black
With silver buttons, buttons, buttons
All down her back, back, back.

- Say the poem again. On the words that repeat, pick your baby up high in the air.

What brain research says

The prime time for language learning is the first few years of life. Children need to hear you talking, singing, and reading to them during these early years. Respond to their babbling and language efforts.

Where Is Teddy?

- Babies usually love to search the floor for dropped objects.
- Play this game with your baby.
- Hold your baby's favorite teddy or stuffed animal in your arms, and then gently drop it to the floor.
- Ask your baby, "Where is teddy?"
- Encourage him to move his body to get the teddy.
- If he's showing you with sounds and gestures that teddy is out of reach, help him get teddy by bringing it close enough for him to grab.
- This builds his confidence.
- When he retrieves it, ask him, "Shall we do it again?"
- Walk around the room, and gently drop teddy to the floor in a different place.
- Keep playing the game as long as your baby is interested.
- Ask him to drop teddy, and you can retrieve it.

What brain research says

Babies need a safe environment to explore in order to develop their motor skills and the brain connections that go with them.

Yes, I Can

- This is a bathtub game. Give your baby her own tightly wrung-out washcloth.
- Make up your own melody, and chant or sing, "Can you wash your face?" Take the baby's hand, and rub the washcloth gently on her face, then sing or chant, "Yes, I can. Yes, I can."
- Continue playing this game as you name all parts of the body: hands, feet, cheek, nose, ears, and so on.
- Next ask the baby to wash your face, your hands, your nose, and so on.
- To dry the baby, play the same game by giving the baby a towel with which to dry herself.

What brain research says

Provide lots of time and opportunities for practice and repetition. Few things build a child's brain and open avenues for learning more than consistent repetition of healthy activities and experiences.

Sink or Float Game

- You can play this game in the bathtub or with a large container filled with water.
  Note: Never leave your baby alone unattended in the bathtub, near a container of water, or near any water source.
- You will also need several items that will sink or float in the water.
- Put one of the floating items in the water, and ask, "See how it floats?"
  - Next put a sinkable item in the water, and say, "Watch it sink to the bottom."
    - Repeat with the remaining items, alternating between the floaters and sinkers.
      - Let your child pick one of the items and start experimenting.
    - Try other toys to see if they will sink or float.

What brain research says

This is a great game to develop cognitive thinking. The growth of babies' brain cell connections depends a lot on their environment and their experiences.

Look Out, Here Comes _____!

- Creating an obstacle course for your baby will develop his coordination and confidence while he learns to crawl and walk.
- You can create a straight-line course by placing pillows and cushions of various heights between two solid barriers such as a couch and a wall.
- Place your baby at one end, and sit at the opposite end with a toy in your hand.
- Say, "Look out, here comes (child's name)!" and encourage him to climb over each pillow and cushion.
- When he reaches you, give him the toy, and say, "Hooray, (child's name) climbed over all the pillows!"

What brain research says

Height awareness and balance are improved with this game. Games that encourage infants to learn control and coordination set the stage for all further development. The neurons are "happy" that these skills have been accomplished.

References and Resources

Books

Bergen, D. and J. Coscia. 2001. *Brain research and early childhood education: Implications for educators*. Olney, MD: Association for Childhood Education International.

Brown, S. 2009. *Play: How it shapes the brain, opens the imagination, and invigorates the soul*. New York: Penguin.

Caine, G. and R. Caine. 2009. *Making connections: Teaching and the human brain*. Chicago: Addison-Wesley.

Carnegie Corporation of New York. 1994. *Starting points: Meeting the needs of our youngest children*. New York: Carnegie Corporation.

Eliot, L. 1999. *What's going on in there? How the brain and mind develop in the first five years of life*. New York: Bantam.

Eliot, L. 2009. *Pink brain, blue brain: How small differences grow into troublesome gaps—and what we can do about It*. New York: Mariner Books.

Elkind, D. 2000. *The power of play: How spontaneous, imaginative activities lead to happier, healthier children*. Cambridge, MA: Da Capo Press.

Gardner, H. 1983. *Frames of mind: The theory of multiple intelligences*. New York: Basic Books.

Gerhardt, S. 2004. *Why love matters: How affection shapes a baby's brain*. New York: Brunner-Routledge.

Goodwin, S. and L. Acredolo. 2005. *Baby hearts: A guide to giving your child an emotional head start*. New York: Bantam.

Gopnik, A., A. N. Meltzoff, P. K. Kuhl. 2000. *The scientist in the crib: What early learning tells us about the mind*. New York: HarperCollins.

Gordon, M. 2005. *The roots of empathy: Changing the world child by child*. Toronto: Thomas Allen Publishers.

Hirsh-Pasek, K. and R. M. Golinkoff. 2004. *Einstein never used flashcards*. Emmaus, PA: Rodale.

Howard, P. J. 1994. *The owners' manual for the brain: Everyday applications from mind-brain research*. Austin, TX: Leornian Press.

Kotulak, R. 1996. *Inside the brain: Revolutionary discoveries of how the mind works*. Kansas City, MO: Andrews and McMeel.

Langer, E. J. 1997. *The power of mindful learning*. Cambridge, MA: Da Capo Press.

Medina, J. 2008. *Brain rules: 12 principles for surviving and thriving at work, home, and school*. Seattle, WA: Pear Press.

Medina, J. 2010. *Brain rules for baby: How to raise a smart and happy child from zero to five*. Seattle, WA: Pear Press.

Riley, D., R.R. San Juan, J. Klinkner, and A. Ramminger. 2008. *Social & emotional development: Connecting science and practice in early childhood settings*. St. Paul, MN: Redleaf Press.

Schiller, P. 1999. *Start smart: Building brain power in the early years*. Beltsville, MD: Gryphon House.

Shore, R. 1997. *Rethinking the brain: New insights into early development*. New York: Families and Work Institute.

Silberg, J. 2001. *Games to play with babies*, 3rd edition. Beltsville, MD: Gryphon House.

Silberg, J. 2002. *Games to play with toddlers*, revised. Beltsville, MD: Gryphon House.

Silberg, J. 2002. *Games to play with two year olds*, revised. Beltsville, MD: Gryphon House.

Silberg, J. 2009. *Baby smarts: games for playing and learning*. Beltsville, MD: Gryphon House.

Sylwester, R. 1995. *A celebration of neurons: An educator's guide to the human brain*. Alexandria, VA: Association for Supervision and Curriculum Development.

Websites

Better Brains for Babies. http://www.fcs.uga.edu/ext/bbb

BrainNet. http://www.brainnet.org

The Dana Foundation. http://www.dana.org/

Talaris Institute. http://www.talaris.org

Zero to Three: National Center for Infants, Toddlers, and Families. http://www.zerotothree.org

DVDs and Videos

Can you pass the all-time great parent test? Chicago: McCormick Tribune Foundation. 49 min.

Brazelton, T. B. 2004. *10 things every child needs for the best start in life*.

Kuhl, P. *The linguistic genius of babies*. Filmed October 2010. TED video, 10:18. Posted February 2011. http://www.ted.com/talks/patricia_kuhl_the_linguistic_genius_of_babies.html

Perry, B. "Dr. Bruce Perry, childhood development on LIVING SMART with Patricia Gras." YouTube video, 26:41, from *Houston PBS Living Smart*, posted by "HoustonPBS," March 15, 2010, http://www.youtube.com/watch?v=vak-iDwZJY8

Reiner, R. *The first years last forever*. From the I Am Your Child video series. Produced by Parents' Action for Children and Rob Reiner. May 1, 2005. DVD, 30 min.

Articles

Caine, R. N., G. Caine, C. L. McClintic, and K. J. Klimek. 2004. 12 Brain/Mind learning principles in action—One author's personal journey. *New Horizons for Learning*.

Highfield, R. 2008. Harvard's baby brain research lab. *The Telegraph*, April 30.

Swidley, N. 2007. Rush, little baby. *Boston Globe*, October 28.

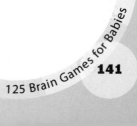

Index